Wild About Wheels

# BUSES

Nancy Dickmann

Raintree is an imprint of Capstone Global Library Limited, a company incorporated in England and Wales having its registered office at 264 Banbury Road, Oxford, OX2 7DY – Registered company number: 6695582

www.raintree.co.uk
myorders@raintree.co.uk

Hardback edition © Capstone Global Library Limited 2022
Paperback edition © Capstone Global Library Limited 2023
The moral rights of the proprietor have been asserted.

All rights reserved. No part of this publication may be reproduced in any form or by any means (including photocopying or storing it in any medium by electronic means and whether or not transiently or incidentally to some other use of this publication) without the written permission of the copyright owner, except in accordance with the provisions of the Copyright, Designs and Patents Act 1988 or under the terms of a licence issued by the Copyright Licensing Agency, 5th Floor, Shackleton House, 4 Battle Bridge Lane, London SE1 2HX (www.cla.co.uk). Applications for the copyright owner's written permission should be addressed to the publisher.

Edited by Amy McDonald Maranville
Designed by Cynthia Della-Rovere
Original illustrations © Capstone Global Library Limited 2022
Picture research by Eric Gohl
Production by Katy LaVigne
Originated by Capstone Global Library Ltd
Printed and bound in India

978 1 3982 2464 3 (hardback)
978 1 3982 2463 6 (paperback)

**British Library Cataloguing in Publication Data**
A full catalogue record for this book is available from the British Library.

**Acknowledgements**
We would like to thank the following for permission to reproduce photographs:
Alamy: keith morris, 17, Wild Places Photography/Chris Howes, 16; Capstone Studio: Karon Dubke, 21 (back); Getty Images: Anadolu Agency/Ali Atmaca, 8; iStockphoto: anilbolukbas, 10, BDMcIntosh, cover, back cover, Drazen, 9; Shutterstock: Ander Dylan, 14, Andrew V Marcus, 18–19, Bikeworldtravel, 11, dade72, 5, Dusan Petkovic, 7, istanbulphotos, 6, Pavel L Photo and Video, 13, RaksyBH, 15, Rawpixel (background), throughout, Snamenski, 21 (front), vaalaa, 12, William Perugini, 4

Every effort has been made to contact copyright holders of material reproduced in this book. Any omissions will be rectified in subsequent printings if notice is given to the publisher.

All the internet addresses (URLs) given in this book were valid at the time of going to press. However, due to the dynamic nature of the internet, some addresses may have changed, or sites may have changed or ceased to exist since publication. While the author and publisher regret any inconvenience this may cause readers, no responsibility for any such changes can be accepted by either the author or the publisher.

# Contents

What buses do................4

Look inside...................8

Look outside ................14

    Bus diagram..............18

    Plan a bus route ...........20

    Glossary .................22

    Find out more.............23

    Index ...................24

Words in **bold** are in the glossary.

# What buses do

You want to go to the library with your family in a big city. It's too far to walk. How can you get there? You can get the bus!

Anyone can ride on a bus. The people riding are called **passengers**. They get on and pay their **fare**. The bus makes lots of stops. Passengers get on and off.

Buses take people where they want to go. Not everyone has a car. Buses help them get to work or school.

A bus can carry many people.
These people do not need to drive cars.
Petrol- or diesel-powered cars **pollute** the air.
With fewer of them, there is less pollution.

# Look inside

The driver sits in the front. There are pedals and a steering wheel. The driver uses them to drive. There are controls to open the doors.

There are different ways to pay the fare. Sometimes you buy a ticket before you get on. You might hand money to the driver. You can even tap a **pass** on a **card reader**.

A bus has lots of seats. Sometimes the bus is very full. Passengers have to stand. They can hold on to bars or straps.

There are buttons by some of the seats. You can push the button. It rings a bell to tell the driver you want to get off. Some buses have a cord to pull instead.

This bus has an **engine** that uses **diesel** fuel. It can cause pollution. Electric buses are cleaner. They have a **battery** and an electric motor inside. The battery needs to be recharged when its power runs low.

A hybrid bus has an electric motor and a diesel engine. The bus uses the electric motor. It can use the diesel engine when the battery needs to be recharged.

# Look outside

Many buses have a ramp. A wheelchair can drive up the ramp. When the chair is inside, the ramp is removed and the doors can close.

Each bus has a sign on the front.

Sometimes there is a sign on the side too.

The sign tells people the **route** number.

It tells people where the bus will go.

15

Many buses run day and night. Buses have headlights. They help the driver to see when it is dark. They help other drivers to see the bus too.

Buses run in all kinds of weather. They have windscreen wipers that wipe the rain away. Now the driver can see the road. He can drive the bus safely.

# Bus diagram

sign

doors

sign

wipers

headlights

19

# Plan a bus route

Imagine you are in charge of a city bus. Where would it go? You can find a map of your area and copy it. Or you can draw one yourself. Label shops, schools and parks. Now plan a route. Where would a bus be most useful? Where will you put the bus stops? Draw them on your map.

21

# Glossary

**battery** container filled with chemicals that produces electrical power

**card reader** machine that reads and checks an electronic pass

**diesel** type of fuel that is made from oil

**engine** machine that makes the power needed to move something

**fare** money that a passenger must pay to travel on a bus or other vehicle

**pass** card that allows a person to travel on a bus

**passenger** person who travels on a bus, train or other vehicle

**pollute** make the air, land or water dirty

**route** road or course followed to get somewhere

# Find out more

## Books

*Buses* (Transport in My Community), Cari Meister (Raintree, 2020)

The *History of Transport* (The History of Technology), Chris Oxlade (Raintree, 2018)

## Websites

**kids.kiddle.co/bus**
Find out more about buses and their history.

**www.bbc.co.uk/iplayer/episode/m000bkbz/graces-amazing-machines-series-1-14-transport-machines**
Watch this CBBC video about buses and other forms of transport.

# Index

bars  10
batteries  12, 13
buttons  11

card readers  9
cars  6, 7
cords  11

doors  8, 14
drivers  8, 9, 11, 16, 17

electric motors  12, 13
engines  12, 13

fares  5, 9

headlights  16

passengers  5, 10
passes  9
pedals  8
pollution  7, 12

rain  17
ramps  14
routes  15

seats  10, 11
signs  15
steering wheels  8
straps  10

wheelchairs  14
windscreen wipers  17